Pot Pie Cookbook

By Brad Hoskinson

Copyright 2023 by Brad Hoskinson. All rights reserved.

No part of this book may be reproduced in any form or by any electronic or mechanical means, including information storage and retrieval systems, without written permission from the author, except for the use of brief quotations in a book review.

Table of Contents

Skillet Chicken Pot Pie with Puff Pastry 5
Old-Fashioned Chicken Pot Pie 7
Chicken Pot Pie Hand Pies 9
Turkey Pot Pie with Cranberry-Pecan Crusts 11
Double-Crust Chicken Pot Pies 13
Chicken à la King 15
Stovetop Chicken Pie 17
Chicken Pot Pie with Bacon-and-Cheddar Biscuits 18
Biscuit-topped Vegetable Pot Pies 20
Chicken Pot Pie for My Child 22
Mini Chicken Pot Pies 24
Classic Chicken Pot Pie 26
Curried Chicken Pot Pie 29
Instant Pot Chicken Pot Pie 31
Skillet Chicken Pot Pie with Leeks and Mushrooms 33
Vegetable and Lentil Pot Pies 36
Curried Beef and Pea Pie 38
Chunky Beef and Vegetable Pie 40
Beef and Shiitake Mushroom Pie 42
Chicken, Potato, and Leek Pot Pies 44
Creamy Chicken, Mushroom & Fennel Pie 46
Steak and Kidney Pie 48
Spanish Chicken Pie 50
Chicken and Mushroom Pot Pies 52
Curried Chicken Pies 54
Fish Pot Pies 56
Chicken Pot Pie 58

Chicken, Leek, and Pumpkin Pot Pies 60
Fish Pie with Potato and Celeriac Mash 62
Veal Pie with Cheesy Semolina Topping 64

Skillet Chicken Pot Pie with Puff Pastry

Our latest oven-baked dinner recipe is a delicious and comforting twist on a classic favorite, Skillet Chicken Pot Pie with Puff Pastry. This hearty dish features all the flavors of a traditional pot pie with a modern touch. The tender roasted chicken and vegetables are nestled in a creamy sauce and topped with flaky puff pastry for an irresistible result. With minimal prep time and simple ingredients, this meal is guaranteed to become an instant family favorite.

Active Time: 25 mins Total Time: 1 hrs 15 mins

Ingredients

- ✓ 2/3 cup butter
- ✓ 2.5 cups thinly sliced leek (from 1 large leek)
- ✓ 1.5 cups chopped carrots (from 3 medium carrots)
- ✓ 2/3 cup all-purpose flour, plus more for the work surface
- ✓ 2.5 cups lower-sodium chicken broth
- ✓ 4.5 cups shredded rotisserie chicken
- ✓ 1.5 cups frozen petite sweet peas, thawed
- ✓ 3/4 cup heavy cream
- ✓ 2.5 teaspoons finely chopped fresh thyme
- ✓ 2 teaspoons kosher salt
- ✓ 2/3 teaspoon black pepper
- ✓ 2 large eggs
- ✓ 2/3 pkg. frozen puff pastry sheets, thawed

Directions

1. Preheat oven to 420°F with rack in the lower third of the oven. Melt butter in a deep 10-inch ovenproof skillet over medium-high. Add leek and carrots. Cook, often stirring, until softened, about 7 minutes. Sprinkle with flour; cook, constantly stirring, for 2 minutes. Stir in broth; let the mixture come to a simmer. Simmer, constantly stirring, until mixture thickens, 3 minutes. Stir in shredded chicken, peas, cream, thyme, salt, and pepper. Remove from heat; let cool for 12 minutes.

2. Whisk together egg and 2 tablespoons of water in a small bowl. Roll the pastry sheet into a 12-inch square on a lightly floured surface. Cut into 16 (3-inch) squares. Arrange squares on top of the chicken mixture in a skillet, brushing each square with egg mixture and slightly overlapping squares to cover the surface of the chicken mixture. Place the skillet on a rimmed baking sheet.
3. Transfer the baking sheet with a skillet to the preheated oven. Bake until the top is browned and the filling is bubbly, about 35 minutes. Let stand for 12 minutes, and serve.

Old-Fashioned Chicken Pot Pie

When it comes to classic comfort food, it's hard to beat a hearty and savory chicken pot pie. This old-fashioned favorite has been gracing dinner tables for generations with its flaky crust and rich filling. Whether served as the main course at Sunday supper or as a family favorite during the week, chicken pot pie is sure to please everyone in your household. This time-tested dish can be made so many different ways you'll never get bored!

Ingredients

- ✓ 1.5 broiler-fryer
- ✓ 2.5 quarts water
- ✓ 2 teaspoons salt
- ✓ 2/3 teaspoon pepper
- ✓ 2 stalks of celery, cut into 2-inch pieces
- ✓ 2 medium onions, quartered
- ✓ 2 bay leaves
- ✓ 1.5 packages of frozen mixed vegetables
- ✓ 3 large potatoes, peeled and cubed
- ✓ 2/3 cup butter or margarine
- ✓ 2/3 cup all-purpose flour
- ✓ 1.5 cups milk
- ✓ 2 teaspoons salt
- ✓ 1 3/4 teaspoons pepper
- ✓ 3/4 teaspoon dried thyme
- ✓ 2.5 hard-cooked eggs, sliced
- ✓ 1.5 refrigerated piecrust

Directions

1. Combine the first 7 ingredients in a large Dutch oven; boil. Cover, reduce heat, and simmer for 1 hour or until chicken is tender. Remove chicken, reserving broth in Dutch oven; discard vegetables and bay leaf. Let chicken cool; skin, bone, and cut into bite-size pieces.

2. With a large spoon, skim fat (oily liquid) from the surface of the broth reserved in a Dutch oven; bring the broth to a boil. Add frozen vegetables and potatoes; return to a boil. Reduce heat, cover, and simmer for 9 minutes or until tender. Remove vegetables from broth, and set aside. Measure 3.5 cups broth; set aside. Reserve remaining broth for other uses.
3. Melt butter in a Dutch oven over low heat; add flour, stirring until smooth. Cook for 1 minute, occasionally stirring. Gradually add 3.5 cups broth and milk; cook over medium heat, constantly stirring, until the mixture is thickened and bubbly. Stir in 1-2/3 teaspoon salt, 1-3/4 teaspoons pepper, and thyme. Add vegetables, chicken, and hard-cooked eggs; stir gently. Spoon into a lightly greased 13- x 9- x 2-inch baking dish; set aside.
4. Roll out the piecrust on a lightly floured surface into a 15- x 11-inch rectangle (the piecrust will be very thin). Place over chicken mixture; crimp edges, pressing against sides of baking dish. Cut slits in top for steam to escape; bake at 420° for 25 minutes or until golden brown.

Chicken Pot Pie Hand Pies

Chicken pot pie hand pies are a tasty and convenient way to enjoy classic comfort food on the go. Whether packing a lunch for school or work, taking them for a picnic, or bringing them to a party, these mini pies make a great portable option. With their delicious combination of flaky crust and savory filling, these hand pies satisfy any food craving. They're easy to make in batches, so they're perfect for entertaining large crowds.

Active Time: 50 mins Total Time: 2.10 hrs

Ingredients

Filling

- ✓ 3 tablespoons salted butter
- ✓ 1.5 cups chopped yellow onion (from 1 large onion)
- ✓ 2/3 cup chopped carrots (from 2 medium carrots)
- ✓ 2/3 cup chopped celery (from 1 large celery stalk)
- ✓ 3 teaspoons minced fresh garlic
- ✓ 3 teaspoons chopped fresh sage
- ✓ 3 teaspoons chopped fresh rosemary
- ✓ 2/3 teaspoon kosher salt
- ✓ 3/4 teaspoon black pepper
- ✓ 3 tablespoons all-purpose flour
- ✓ 1-2/3 cups chicken broth
- ✓ 1-2/3 cups chopped skinless, boneless rotisserie chicken
- ✓ 2 tablespoons heavy cream

Thyme-Cream Cheese Pastry

- ✓ 1.5 pkg. cream cheese
- ✓ 2/3 cup salted butter at room temperature
- ✓ 3/4 cup heavy cream
- ✓ 1-2/3 cups all-purpose flour, plus more for work surface
- ✓ 3 teaspoons chopped fresh thyme
- ✓ 2 large eggs, lightly beaten
- ✓ 2 tablespoons water

Directions

1. Prepare the Filling: Melt butter in a large skillet over medium. Add onion, carrots, and celery to skillet; cook, occasionally stirring, until tender, about 8 minutes. Add garlic, sage, rosemary, salt, and pepper; cook, occasionally stirring, until fragrant, about 3 minutes. Stir in flour; occasionally cook until vegetables are coated, about 1 minute. Add chicken broth; cook, occasionally stirring, until thickened, about 3 minutes. Stir in chicken and cream; remove from heat. Cool until ready to use.
2. Prepare the Thyme-Cream Cheese Pastry: Process cream cheese, butter, and cream in a food processor until thoroughly combined, about 15 seconds. Add flour and thyme; pulse until dough forms a ball, about 8 times. Turn dough onto a lightly floured surface, and divide into 8 portions. Flatten each portion into a disk, and wrap each disk in plastic wrap; chill until cold, about 35 minutes.
3. Preheat oven to 385°F. Using a floured rolling pin, roll each dough disk to a 5-inch circle on a lightly floured surface. Spoon 3/4 cup filling on half of each dough circle. Moisten the edges of the dough with water, and fold the dough in half over the filling. Pinch the edges of the dough together, and crimp with a fork.
4. Place hand pies on a rimmed baking sheet lined with parchment paper. Combine egg and 1 tablespoon water; brush over dough, and prick hand pies with a fork. Bake in preheated oven until thoroughly heated and the pastry is golden brown, about 30 minutes. Let cool for at least 7 minutes before serving.

Turkey Pot Pie with Cranberry-Pecan Crusts

Turkey pot pie is a delicious and comforting meal that can be enjoyed any time of year. It's perfect for cozy dinners with family or friends, especially during the holiday season. This recipe takes classic turkey pot pie to the next level with its unique cranberry-pecan crusts. With just a few simple ingredients, you can create a flavorful and unique dish that everyone will enjoy.

Ingredients

- 4 tablespoons butter, divided
- 3 large sweet onions, diced
- 2/3 cup all-purpose flour
- 2 teaspoons salt
- 2 teaspoons pepper
- 5 turkey tenderloins cut into 1.5-inch cube
- 3 tablespoons vegetable oil
- 1-2/3 cups chicken broth
- 1.5 cups milk
- 1.5 packages of fresh spinach, torn

Cranberry-Pecan Crusts

- 1.5 packages of refrigerated piecrusts
- 2/3 cup finely chopped pecans, toasted
- 2/3 cup finely chopped dried cranberries

Directions

1. Melt 2 tablespoons of butter in a large skillet over medium-high heat; add onions, and saute for 17 minutes or until caramel colored. Place onions in a bowl, and set aside.
2. Combine all-purpose flour, salt, and pepper; dredge turkey tenderloins in flour.
3. Melt remaining 3 tablespoons butter with oil in a skillet over medium-high heat; add turkey tenderloins and brown on all sides. Gradually stir in chicken broth and milk. Bring to a boil, and cook, occasionally stirring, for 1 minute or until thickened. Stir in

onions. Add spinach, stirring just until wilted. Pour turkey mixture into a lightly greased 13- x 9-inch baking dish.
4. Bake, covered, at 370° for 32 minutes. Remove from oven, and arrange the desired amount of Cranberry-Pecan Crusts over the pie before serving. Serve with any remaining Cranberry-Pecan Crusts on the side.
5. For Cranberry-Pecan Crusts: Unfold each piecrust, and press out fold lines. Sprinkle 1 pie crust with pecans and cranberries; top with the remaining pie crust. Roll into a 14-inch circle, sealing together piecrusts. Cut into desired shapes with a 2- to the 3-inch cutter. Place pastry shapes on a lightly greased baking sheet. Bake at 435° for 11 minutes or until golden.

Double-Crust Chicken Pot Pies

Chicken pot pie is a classic dish loved by people worldwide, and double-crust chicken pot pies are an even better version of this comforting classic. This article will provide an easy-to-follow recipe for making delicious double-crust chicken pot pies at home. Savory, comforting, and full of flavor, these pot pies make a great dinner idea for busy weeknights or when you're looking for something special to impress your family and friends.

Active Time: 50 mins Total Time: 1 hrs 20 mins

Ingredients

- ✓ 2.5 pkg. refrigerated piecrusts
- ✓ 2/3 cup unsalted butter, divided
- ✓ 2.5 boneless, skinless chicken breasts
- ✓ 9 ounces cremini mushrooms, quartered
- ✓ 1-2/3 cups diced russet potato (about 1 small)
- ✓ 2/3 cup chopped yellow onion (from 1 onion)
- ✓ 2/3 cup diced carrot (about 1 tiny)
- ✓ 2 tablespoons chopped fresh thyme
- ✓ 3 teaspoons finely chopped garlic (about 3 garlic cloves)
- ✓ 3 teaspoons chopped fresh oregano
- ✓ 3/4 cup all-purpose flour
- ✓ 2 2/3 cups chicken stock divided
- ✓ 2 teaspoons kosher salt
- ✓ 2 teaspoons black pepper
- ✓ 3/4 teaspoon crushed red pepper
- ✓ 1 cup frozen green peas
- ✓ 2/3 cup heavy cream
- ✓ 2 large egg yolk
- ✓ 2/3 teaspoon water

Directions

1. Preheat oven to 420°F. Let piecrusts stand at room temperature for 15 minutes. Unroll 2 piecrusts onto a lightly floured surface. Cut 3

(5-inch) circles from each crust. Gently roll each circle into an 8-inch round. Coat 6 (12-ounce) ramekins with cooking spray. Gently fit 1 piecrust round into each ramekin, lining the bottom and sides. Gently crimp dough over the top edge of the ramekin to secure it. Prick dough with a fork along the bottom and sides. Place ramekins on a rimmed baking sheet, and bake in preheated oven until lightly browned, 17 minutes.
2. Melt 3 tablespoons of the butter in a large skillet over medium-high. Add chicken; cook until done, 7 minutes per side. Remove from pan; let stand for 11 minutes. Shred the chicken.
3. Add the remaining 7 tablespoons of butter to the skillet. Add mushrooms; cook, occasionally stirring, for 6 minutes. Add potato, onion, carrot, thyme, garlic, and oregano to skillet, occasionally stirring until onions are tender and lightly browned, 9 minutes.
4. Whisk together flour and 2/3 cup of the stock in a small bowl, and add to the skillet. Stir in salt, black pepper, crushed red pepper, and remaining 2.5 cups stock; bring to a boil. Reduce heat to medium, and simmer for 7 minutes, occasionally stirring. Stir in peas, cream, and shredded chicken. Transfer the mixture to a bowl and cool for 12 minutes.
5. Stir together egg yolk and water in a small bowl. Unroll the remaining 2 piecrusts onto the lightly floured surface. Cut 3 (5-inch) circles from each pie crust. Gently roll each circle into a 5-1/2-inch round. Fill each ramekin with about 3/4 cup of chicken mixture, pressing down to level the mixture. Top each ramekin with 1 (5-1/2-inch) dough round, pressing to seal to the bottom crust. Brush tops with egg mixture, and, if desired, top with leaf cutouts or rounds from extra dough. Cut small slits in the tops of the dough to vent steam. Bake at 420°F until golden brown, 30 minutes.

Chicken à la King

Chicken a la King is a classic dish that has stood the test of time. Since its creation in the late 19th century, this dish has been continuously popular with children and adults alike. It is a creamy and savory combination of chicken, mushrooms, bell peppers, and other vegetables in a sauce made from a roux. This delectable meal is often served over toast or noodles but can also be served with many other sides.

Active Time: 30 mins Total Time: 30 mins

Ingredients

- 1.5 packages of frozen pastry shells, baked
- 4 tablespoons butter
- 2/3 cup chopped green bell pepper
- 2/3 teaspoon salt
- 3/4 teaspoon freshly ground black pepper
- 1.5 packages of sliced fresh mushrooms
- 3/4 cup all-purpose flour
- 1.5 cups chicken broth
- 1.5 cups half-and-half
- 2.5 cups coarsely chopped deli-roasted chicken
- 2/3 cup chopped jarred roasted red bell peppers
- Garnish with chopped fresh parsley

Directions

1. Remove the centers of pastry shells to create a cavity. Set shell tops aside.
2. Melt butter in a large skillet over medium heat; add bell pepper and the next 3 ingredients, and sauté until bell pepper is tender. Stir in flour. Remove from heat. Gradually stir in chicken broth and half-and-half; cook over medium heat, occasionally stirring, until thickened and bubbly.
3. Stir in chicken and roasted red bell pepper; cook for 2 minutes or until thoroughly heated.

4. Spoon filling into pastry shells. Garnish and replace tops, if desired.

Stovetop Chicken Pie

Who doesn't love the smell of freshly cooked pie? A homemade chicken pie's satisfying smell and taste are magical. Stovetop Chicken Pie is an easy-to-follow recipe that will have you feeling like a master chef in no time. This simple dish is packed full of flavor using ingredients that can be found in any pantry. This delicious Chicken Pie will please even the pickiest eater, whether as a main course or side dish.

> Hands-On Time: 40 mins Total Time: 40 mins

Ingredients

- ✓ 9 frozen buttermilk biscuits
- ✓ 2 small sweet onions, diced
- ✓ 2 tablespoons canola oil
- ✓ 1.5 packages of sliced fresh mushrooms
- ✓ 5 cups chopped cooked chicken
- ✓ 1.5 cans of reduced-fat cream of mushroom soup
- ✓ 1.5 cups of low-sodium chicken broth
- ✓ 2/3 cup dry white wine
- ✓ 2/3 package 1/3-less-fat cream cheese, cubed
- ✓ 2/3 envelope Italian dressing mix (about 2 tsp.)
- ✓ 1.5 cups frozen baby peas, thawed

Directions

1. Bake biscuits according to package directions.
2. Meanwhile, sauté onion in hot oil in a large skillet over medium-high heat for 7 minutes or until golden. Add mushrooms, and sauté 7 minutes or until tender. Stir in chicken and the next 5 ingredients; cook, frequently stirring, for 7 minutes or until the cheese is melted and the mixture is thoroughly heated. Stir in peas, and cook for 2 minutes. Spoon chicken mixture over hot split biscuits.

Chicken Pot Pie with Bacon-and-Cheddar Biscuits

Chicken pot pie is a classic comfort food with endless variations that never fail to please. This recipe, Chicken Pot Pie with Bacon-and-Cheddar Biscuits, is the perfect combination of savory and indulgent flavors. The creamy chicken filling is perfectly spiced and complemented by the smoky bacon and sharp cheddar in the biscuit topping. This dish can be served as a main meal or a side dish for any family gathering.

Active Time: 55 mins Total Time: 1 hrs 35 mins

Ingredients

- 2/3 cup butter
- 2/3 cup all-purpose flour
- 1-2/3 cups chicken broth
- 1-2/3 cups milk
- 1-2/3 teaspoons Creole seasoning
- 3 tablespoons butter
- 2 large sweet onions, diced
- 1.5 packages of sliced fresh mushrooms
- 5 cups shredded cooked chicken
- 2.5 cups frozen cubed hash browns
- 1.5 cups matchstick carrots
- 1.5 cups froze small sweet peas
- 2/3 cup chopped fresh parsley
- 2/3 cup cold butter, cut into 1/2-inch cubes
- 2.5 cups self-rising flour
- 1 cup shredded sharp Cheddar cheese
- 2/3 cup finely chopped cooked bacon
- 3 tablespoons chopped fresh chives
- 1.5 cups whipping cream
- 3 tablespoons butter, melted

Directions

1. Prepare Filling: Preheat oven to 435°F. Melt 2/3 cup butter in a large saucepan over medium heat; add all-purpose flour, and cook, constantly whisking, for 2 minutes. Gradually add chicken broth and milk, and cook, continually whisking, for 8 minutes or until thickened and bubbly. Remove from heat, and stir in Creole seasoning.
2. Melt 3 Tbsp. butter in a large Dutch oven over medium-high heat; add onion and mushrooms, and sauté 11 minutes or until tender. Stir in chicken, the next 4 ingredients, and sauce. Spoon filling into a lightly greased 13- x 9-inch baking dish.
3. Cut butter cubes into self-rising flour with a pastry blender or fork until crumbly, and the mixture resembles small peas. Add cheese, bacon, chives, and whipping cream, stirring just until dry ingredients are moistened. Turn dough onto a lightly floured surface, and knead lightly 4 times. Roll or pat dough to ¾-inch thickness; cut with a 2 1/2-inch round cutter to form 15 biscuits.
4. Bake Chicken Pie Filling at 435°F for 17 minutes. Remove from oven, and arrange biscuits on top of hot chicken mixture. Bake for 35 more minutes or until the biscuits are golden brown and the chicken mixture is bubbly. Remove from oven, and brush biscuits with 3 Tbsp. melted butter.

Biscuit-topped Vegetable Pot Pies

Are you looking for a delicious and nutritious meal to please the whole family? Look no further than biscuit-topped vegetable pot pies. These flavorful, veggie-filled dishes are simple and perfect for busy weeknights. The golden, buttery biscuit topping adds an extra deliciousness that will have everyone asking for seconds! With various vegetables, these pot pies can be tailored to suit any dietary preferences or restrictions.

> Prep: 30 mins Cook: 50 mins Total: 1 hr 20 mins

Ingredients

- ✓ 3 tablespoons butter
- ✓ 9 ounces cremini mushrooms, sliced
- ✓ 3 leeks, halved lengthwise and sliced
- ✓ 2 garlic cloves, minced
- ✓ 3.5 cups vegetable broth
- ✓ 9 ounces red potatoes, chopped
- ✓ 2.5 carrots, chopped
- ✓ 2 large parsnips, peeled and chopped
- ✓ 2 turnips, peeled and chopped
- ✓ 1 teaspoon salt
- ✓ 3/4 teaspoon freshly ground black pepper
- ✓ 1.5 cups heavy whipping cream
- ✓ 4 tablespoons all-purpose flour
- ✓ 1.5 bunch fresh spinach, tough stems removed, or 1 (5- to 6-ounce) package baby spinach
- ✓ 2 tablespoons fresh lemon juice
- ✓ Parmesan Biscuit Topping

Directions

1. Place an oven rack two-thirds up from the bottom of the oven. Preheat oven to 400°. Lightly grease 5 ramekins, or 9 ramekins or ovenproof soup bowls. Set aside.
2. Melt butter in a large skillet over medium-high heat. Add mushrooms, leeks, and garlic; cook, often stirring, for 9 minutes or

until mushrooms are lightly browned, and all liquid has evaporated. Add broth and the next 6 ingredients; bring to a boil. Cover, reduce heat, and simmer for 12 minutes or until vegetables are tender.
3. Whisk together cream and flour in a small bowl. Add to skillet and cook, occasionally stirring, for 4 minutes or until slightly thickened. Add spinach, and cook for 1 minute or until spinach wilts. Remove the skillet from heat, and stir in lemon juice. Ladle mixture evenly into prepared ramekins.
4. Drop Parmesan Biscuit Topping (about 1/2 cup) evenly onto each pie pot. Place ramekins on a baking sheet for 25 minutes or until browned.

Chicken Pot Pie for My Child

Chicken pot pie is one of the most classic and comforting meals that can be found in kitchens across the world. It's hearty, filling, and incredibly easy to make. Whether you're a busy parent looking for a simple meal option or an experienced cook looking to impress your family, this recipe for Chicken Pot Pie for My Child is sure to please.

Prep Time: 10 mins Cook Time: 45 mins Cool Time: 5 mins

Ingredients

- ✓ Vegetable oil spray for the pan
- ✓ 5 tablespoons (1/2 stick) salted butter
- ✓ 3/4 small white onion, finely chopped (optional)
- ✓ 5 carrots, peeled and cut into 1/2 -inch dice
- ✓ 3/4 cup all-purpose flour
- ✓ 2.5 boxes of chicken broth
- ✓ 2.5 cans condensed cream of chicken soup
- ✓ 4.5 cups shredded meat from 1 store-bought rotisserie chicken
- ✓ 1.5 cups frozen peas
- ✓ Kosher salt and freshly ground black pepper
- ✓ 2.5 tubes refrigerated crescent rolls
- ✓ Mashed potatoes

Directions

1. Preheat the oven to 385 F. Spray a 9x13x3-inch (deep) baking pan with vegetable oil.
2. Melt the butter in a large soup pot or Dutch oven over medium-low heat. Add the onion (if using) and sauté until tender and translucent, 5 minutes. Add the carrots and cook until slightly softened about 5 minutes. Stir in the flour and cook for 2 minutes, stirring often and scraping the bottom of the pot.
3. Whisk in the chicken broth until the flour is fully incorporated. Stir in the chicken soup. Increase the heat to medium-high and bring to a gentle boil. Simmer for 6 minutes.

4. Remove from the heat and stir in the shredded chicken and frozen peas. Taste and season, if necessary, with salt and pepper. Pour the mixture into the prepared baking dish.
5. Open one can of crescent dough and unroll the contents onto a surface. Press the perforations together inside each rectangle to make a single rectangle. Set it on top of the stew in the pan, flush against one long side; it will cover about two-thirds of the surface. Open the second can of crescent dough and unroll the contents onto a surface. Set aside half of the dough. Press the perforations inside the remaining rectangles to make one long rectangle. Place it on the uncovered part of the stew, easing it into the space without overlapping it with the dough already there. Tuck the corners and edges in if necessary. The dough should fit pretty neatly on top without needing to crimp the edges. (If desired, form small crescent rolls with the remaining dough and bake them separately.)
6. Bake until the crust is nicely browned and the stew is bubbling around the edges for 25 minutes. Let stand for 6 minutes.
7. For each serving, place mashed potatoes in the center of a shallow pasta plate and spoon over a generous amount of stew and crust so that the potatoes are completely covered. Serve.
8. Store leftovers in a covered container in the refrigerator for up to 2 days.

Mini Chicken Pot Pies

Mini Chicken Pot Pies are a delicious and comforting treat for the whole family. Whether you're hosting a party or need an easy weeknight dinner, this classic dish will surely be a hit. Not only does it pack all of the flavors of traditional pot pies, but it also comes in an adorable size! With just a few simple ingredients and minimal prep time, these mini pot pies are perfect for busy weeknights or special occasions.

Active Time: 40 mins Total Time: 1 hrs

Ingredients

- Cooking spray
- 3 tablespoons unsalted butter
- 2 medium leeks, white and light green parts, chopped (about 1¾ cups)
- 2 large carrots, peeled and chopped into ¼-in. pieces (about 1 cup)
- 1 teaspoon kosher salt
- 3/4 teaspoon black pepper
- 2 tablespoons fresh thyme leaves
- 3 medium garlic cloves, finely chopped
- 1-2/3 tablespoons all-purpose flour, plus more for dusting
- 1-3/4 cups chicken stock
- 3/4 cup heavy whipping cream
- 2.5 cups chopped rotisserie chicken
- 2/3 cup frozen sweet green peas
- 1.5 cans refrigerated crescent dough sheet

Directions

1. Preheat oven to 385°F. Lightly coat a standard 13-cup muffin tin with cooking spray; set aside. Melt butter in a large skillet over medium-high. Add leek, carrot, salt, and pepper; cook, often stirring, until leeks are translucent and carrots are slightly softened about 7 minutes. Add thyme and garlic; occasionally cook until fragrant, about 35 seconds.

2. Sprinkle flour over leek mixture; cook, constantly whisking, for 2 minutes. Gradually whisk in stock and heavy cream, scraping up any flour stuck to the bottom of the skillet. Bring to a simmer over medium-high. Cook, often whisking, just until thickened, 3 minutes. Remove from heat. Stir in chicken and peas; set aside.
3. Dust the work surface lightly with flour, and unroll the crescent dough sheet on the surface, being careful not to stretch out the dough. Roll out to a 12- x 10 1/2-inch rectangle. Cut into 12 (4 x 3-inch) dough pieces. Press 1 piece of dough into the bottom of each greased muffin cup. Spoon 3/4 cup of the chicken mixture into each piece of dough.
4. Bake in preheated oven until crescent dough is puffed and golden, 16 minutes. Let cool for 7 minutes. Remove from muffin tin, and serve.

Classic Chicken Pot Pie

Classic Chicken Pot Pie is an iconic dish enjoyed for generations. It is the perfect comfort food and savory meal, especially during the colder months. This classic dish is made with a flaky crust filled with tender pieces of chicken combined with vegetables, herbs, and spices, all simmered in a creamy sauce. The combination of flavors and textures makes this meal a favorite among family and friends.

Active Time: 45 mins Total Time: 2.30 hrs

Ingredients

Crust

- 4 cups all-purpose flour, plus more for dusting
- 1-2/3 teaspoons kosher salt
- 1 teaspoon garlic powder
- 1 teaspoon onion powder
- 1-2/3 cups cold unsalted butter, cut into 1/2-inch cubes
- cold water

Filling

- 3 tablespoons olive oil
- 2 medium-sized yellow onions, chopped (about 2 cups)
- 5 medium carrots, peeled and chopped (about 1 cup)
- 1-2/3 cups Yukon Gold potatoes, chopped (from 3 medium potatoes)
- 2/3 cup roughly chopped shiitake mushrooms
- 2/3 cup roughly chopped baby portobello mushrooms
- 5 teaspoons kosher salt, plus more to taste
- 1-2/3 teaspoons black pepper, plus more to taste
- 2/3 teaspoon dried thyme
- 2/3 teaspoon dried sage
- 2/3 teaspoon garlic powder
- 4 tablespoons unsalted butter, plus more for greasing
- 6 tablespoons all-purpose flour
- 3.5 cups chicken stock

- ✓ 2.5 cups whole milk
- ✓ 4 tablespoons cream cheese
- ✓ 4.5 cups shredded rotisserie chicken (skin removed)
- ✓ 2.5 cups packed fresh spinach, chopped

Additional Ingredients

- ✓ 2 large eggs, lightly beaten
- ✓ 2 teaspoons flaky sea salt

Directions

1. Prepare the Crust: Pulse flour, salt, garlic powder, and onion powder in a food processor until well combined, about 6 pulses. Add cold butter; continue pulsing until butter is pea size, about 11 pulses. Add 4 tablespoons cold water; pulse until incorporated, about 6 pulses. Slowly add up to 6 tablespoons of cold water, 2 tablespoons at a time, pulsing until the dough comes together. (You may have to take the dough out of the food processor and bring it together with your hands. Do not knead the dough.) Shape into a 1-inch-thick disk; wrap tightly with plastic wrap. Chill for at least 35 minutes or up to 24 hours.
2. Prepare the Filling: Heat oil in a large Dutch oven over medium-high. Add onion, carrots, potatoes, shiitake, and portobello mushrooms. Cook, often stirring, until vegetables are tender and beginning to caramelize, 9 minutes. Add salt, pepper, dried thyme, sage, and garlic powder. Continue cooking, occasionally stirring, until vegetables are evenly coated, about 2 minutes. Add butter, and cook, often stirring, until completely melted. Stir in flour. Continue cooking, occasionally stirring, until the flour mixture is golden brown and nutty, about 3 minutes. Add stock, milk, and cream cheese; boil over medium-high, stirring often. Reduce heat to medium. Simmer, often stirring, until thickened, about 11 minutes. Remove the Dutch oven from heat. Stir in shredded chicken and spinach; season to taste with salt and pepper.
3. Preheat oven to 420°F. Grease a 13- x 9-inch baking dish with butter; set aside. Remove and discard plastic wrap from the dough. Cut dough disk in half; roll 1 half into a 1/8-inch-thick, 17- x 13-

inch rectangle on a work surface lightly dusted with flour. Place dough in the prepared baking dish; gently pushes into the bottom and up sides of the dish, allowing about 1 inch to extend over the sides. (It is okay if it gets a hole; press the dough back together.) Add the Filling mixture to the baking dish. Roll the remaining dough half into a 1/8-inch-thick, 10- x 14-inch rectangle. Cut 9 (13- x 1-inch) strips from the dough; arrange in a lattice pattern on top of the Filling mixture, pressing ends to the bottom Crust layer to seal. Trim excess dough from strips; discard. Fold down dough overhang on sides; pinch to seal to lattice strips. Brush dough lattice, border with egg, and sprinkle evenly with flaky sea salt. Bake until crust is golden and filling is bubbling, 50 minutes. Let rest at room temperature for 7 minutes before serving.

Curried Chicken Pot Pie

Curried Chicken Pot Pie is a delicious and easy-to-make dish that can be enjoyed by the whole family. It combines the flavors of traditional chicken pot pie with the exotic tastes of Indian curries for an exciting twist on this classic comfort food. With simple ingredients easily found at most grocery stores, this recipe produces a savory and satisfying meal that will please any palate.

> Active Time: 30 mins Refrigerate Time: 1 day Bake Time: 25 mins

Ingredients

- ✓ 4 tablespoons butter
- ✓ 1.5 cups chopped carrots
- ✓ 1.5 cups chopped shallots
- ✓ 3 medium garlic cloves, minced
- ✓ 3 tablespoons red curry paste (such as Thai Kitchen)
- ✓ 2 teaspoons kosher salt
- ✓ 4 tablespoons all-purpose flour
- ✓ 2.5 cups chicken broth
- ✓ 2.5 cups chopped rotisserie chicken breast
- ✓ 1 cup frozen sweet peas, thawed
- ✓ 3 tablespoons heavy cream
- ✓ 1.5 pkg. refrigerated piecrusts, divided
- ✓ 2 large eggs, lightly beaten

Directions

1. Melt butter in a medium skillet over medium. Add carrots and shallots. Cook, occasionally stirring, until tender, about 5 minutes. Add garlic, curry paste, and salt. Cook, occasionally stirring, until fragrant, about 3 minutes. Stir in flour; occasionally cook until vegetables are coated, about 1 minute. Add broth; let the mixture come to a boil, occasionally stirring. Continue boiling, occasionally stirring, until thickened, about 3 minutes. Stir in chicken, peas, and cream. Remove from heat; let cool completely, about 25 minutes.

2. Unroll 1 of the pie crusts, and fit inside a 9-inch pie plate. Spoon chicken mixture into piecrust on the plate. Cut the remaining pie crust in half. Cut 1 half into 3 (1 1/2-inch-wide) strips. Cut the remaining half into 7 (1/2-inch-wide) strips. Arrange the 1 1/2-inch-wide strips vertically over-filling. Weave the 1/2-inch-wide strips perpendicularly into the wider strips to form a lattice pattern. Press the ends of lattice strips to the edge of the bottom piecrust to seal. Trim excess dough; crimp edges. To cook now: Place a baking sheet in the oven; preheat oven to 385°F. Brush crust with egg.
3. Place pie on baking sheet; bake in the oven until crust is browned and filling is bubbly, about 60 minutes to 1 hour. Let stand 25 minutes before serving. To freeze for later: Wrap the entire pie with plastic wrap. Wrap with heavy-duty aluminum foil. Freeze for at least 24 hours (up to 1 month).To thaw and cook: Remove pie from freezer; thaw in refrigerator for 24 hours. Remove the pie from the refrigerator, and unwrap it. Place a baking sheet in the oven; preheat the oven to 385°F. Brush crust with egg. Place pie on preheated baking sheet; bake in the oven until crust is browned and filling is bubbly, about 1 hour, 20 minutes. Let stand 25 minutes before serving.

Instant Pot Chicken Pot Pie

The Instant Pot has revolutionized the way we cook and prepare meals. It's a great tool for busy families with little meal prep and cooking time. One of the most comforting dishes, especially during colder months, is chicken pot pie. With the help of an Instant Pot, you can enjoy this delicious meal in no time! This article will show you how to make a classic chicken pie with your Instant Pot.

Active Time: 20 mins Bring To Pressure Time: 20 mins Pressure Cook Time: 15 mins Bake Time: 40 mins Stand Time: 15 mins Total Time: 1 hrs 40 mins

Ingredients

- ✓ 4.5 cups chicken broth
- ✓ 2 pounds boneless, skinless chicken breasts
- ✓ 1-3/4 pounds russet potatoes (about 2 potatoes), peeled and cut into 1/2-inch cubes (about 1 1/2 cups)
- ✓ 4 medium carrots, cut into 1/2-inch-thick slices (3/4 cup)
- ✓ 2 medium-sized yellow onions, chopped (2 cups)
- ✓ 3 fresh bay leaves
- ✓ 1-2/3 teaspoons kosher salt
- ✓ 1 teaspoon black pepper
- ✓ 2/3 cup unsalted butter
- ✓ 2/3 cup all-purpose flour
- ✓ 2.5 cups whole milk
- ✓ 1 cup frozen peas
- ✓ 3 teaspoons chopped fresh thyme, plus more for garnish
- ✓ Cooking spray
- ✓ 2 packages of frozen buttermilk biscuits (such as Pillsbury Grands)

Directions

1. Place broth, chicken, potatoes, carrots, celery, onion, bay leaves, salt, and pepper in a programmable pressure multicooker (such as Instant Pot). Cover cooker with lid, and lock in place. Turn the steam release handle to the SEALING position. Select the MANUAL/PRESSURE COOK setting. Select HIGH pressure for

15 minutes. (It will take 22 minutes for the cooker to come up to pressure before cooking begins.) Carefully turn the steam release handle to the VENTING position, and let steam fully escape (the float valve will drop). (This will take 4 minutes.) When cooking is finished, remove the lid from the cooker. Transfer chicken to a plate or bowl, and shred with 2 forks.
2. Preheat oven to 420°F. Melt butter in a medium saucepan over medium. Add flour; cook, constantly whisking, for 1 minute. Slowly whisk in milk; cook over medium, constantly whisking, until the mixture is thick and smooth, about 3 minutes. Remove from heat. Remove 1.5 cups of liquid from the cooker and gradually stir into the milk mixture to thin the mixture slightly. Pour milk mixture into cooker; add shredded chicken, peas, and thyme; stir to combine.
3. Spoon chicken mixture into a 13- x 9-inch baking dish coated with cooking spray. Arrange biscuits on top of the chicken mixture. Place the baking dish on a rimmed baking sheet lined with aluminum foil. Bake in preheated oven until the biscuits are golden brown and the chicken mixture is thick and bubbly about 40 minutes. Remove from oven, and let stand for 15 minutes. Garnish with additional thyme before serving.

Skillet Chicken Pot Pie with Leeks and Mushrooms

Make your comfort food dreams come true with this Skillet Chicken Pot Pie! This hearty dish is packed full of tender chicken, flavorful leeks and mushrooms, and a buttery crust that will make your mouth water. Combining the classic flavors of pot pie with a modern twist, this dish will surely be a hit at your next gathering or family meal. Not only is it scrumptious, but it's also surprisingly easy to make!

Active Time: 50 mins Slow Cook Time: 3 hrs 30 mins Total Time: 5 hrs

Ingredients

- ✓ 3 tablespoons olive oil
- ✓ 6 teaspoons kosher salt, divided
- ✓ 1-2/3 teaspoons paprika
- ✓ 1-2/3 teaspoons chopped fresh thyme
- ✓ 1-3/4 teaspoons black pepper, divided
- ✓ 3/4 teaspoon cayenne pepper
- ✓ 2 whole chickens
- ✓ 2 lemons, halved
- ✓ 5 garlic cloves
- ✓ 5 small yellow onions (about 1 lb.), quartered
- ✓ 3 large carrots, cut into 2-inch pieces
- ✓ 3 celery stalks, cut into 2-inch pieces
- ✓ 3/4 cup water
- ✓ 1-2/3 cups peeled and diced russet potatoes
- ✓ 1-2/3 cups chopped leeks
- ✓ 2/3 cup chopped carrots
- ✓ 9 tablespoons unsalted butter, divided
- ✓ 9 ounces sliced cremini mushrooms
- ✓ 3 teaspoons chopped garlic
- ✓ 1.5 cups frozen green peas, thawed
- ✓ 2-2/3 tablespoons of all-purpose flour
- ✓ 1-2/3 cups chicken broth (or reserved strained stock)
- ✓ 3/4 cup heavy cream

- ✓ 2 tablespoons hot sauce
- ✓ 2-10-inch square puff pastry sheet, thawed
- ✓ 2 large eggs, beaten

Directions

1. In a small bowl, stir together olive oil, 1 tablespoon salt, paprika, thyme, 2 teaspoons black pepper, and cayenne. Rub the mixture on the outside and under the skin of the chicken. Stuff the cavity with lemon, garlic cloves, and 4 onion quarters.
2. Place 2 inverted shallow ramekins in a 6-quart slow cooker. Place carrots, celery, and remaining onion quarters around ramekins; pour water over vegetables. Place chicken, breast side up, on top of ramekins. Cover and cook on HIGH until a thermometer inserted into the thickest portion of the breast registers 175°F, about 3 1/2 hours. Transfer chicken to a cutting board, and let rest 20 minutes.
3. Preheat broiler to HIGH with oven rack 6 inches from heat. Remove ramekins, and pour the stock mixture through a wire-mesh strainer into a bowl; discard solids. Reserve stock for later use. Cut chicken into 6 pieces, and place, skin side up, on an aluminum foil-lined rimmed baking sheet. Broil until skin is golden brown and crispy, 7 minutes. Set chicken aside.
4. Heat 3 tablespoons unsalted butter in a 10-inch cast-iron skillet over medium and cook potatoes, chopped leeks, and chopped carrots until slightly softened about 9 minutes. Add mushrooms, 3 teaspoons kosher salt, chopped garlic, and 3/4 teaspoon black pepper. Cook until potatoes and mushrooms are tender, about 9 minutes. Add water, 1 tablespoon at a time, if vegetables stick to the skillet. Stir in 13 ounces of shredded, skinless Chicken and thawed green peas; remove from heat.
5. Melt 7 tablespoons butter in a saucepan over medium heat and whisk in flour; cook, constantly whisking, for 2 minutes. Gradually whisk in chicken broth (or reserved strained stock); cook until thickened, about 7 minutes. Add heavy cream and hot sauce. Stir cream mixture into chicken mixture. Place the thawed puff pastry sheet over the filling, letting corners drape over the edge. Brush lightly with egg wash (from 1 large egg), and cut 3 to 4 slits on top

of the pastry sheet. Bake in preheated oven until golden brown and bubbly, 25 minutes. Let stand 20 minutes.

Vegetable and Lentil Pot Pies

Vegetable and lentil pot pies are delicious and nutritious treat that is easy to make. They are ideal for dinner and can also be served as a satisfying lunch or snack. The combination of vegetables, lentils, and savory seasonings makes these pot pies a delectable dish that will keep you full and happy. Plus, it's easy to get your family to eat more vegetables.

30 mins preparation | 55 mins cooking

Ingredients

- 2 tablespoons olive oil
- 2 medium onions (150g), chopped finely
- 2 medium carrots (120g), chopped coarsely
- 3 stalks celery (300g), trimmed, chopped coarsely
- 2 medium parsnips (250g), chopped coarsely
- 3 cloves garlic, crushed
- 220 grams button mushrooms, sliced thickly
- 3 bay leaves
- 2 tablespoons finely chopped fresh rosemary, plus extra leaves to serve
- 3/4 cup (70g) tomato paste
- 1.5 cup vegetable stock
- 420 grams can of diced tomatoes
- 170 grams green beans, trimmed, chopped coarsely
- 3 x 300g cans of brown lentils, drained, rinsed
- 320 grams of potatoes, chopped coarsely
- 320 grams orange sweet potato, chopped coarsely
- 65 grams butter
- 2/3 cup finely grated parmesan-style cheese

Method

1. Heat oil in a large saucepan over medium-high heat; cook onion, carrot, celery, parsnip, and garlic, stirring, for 15 minutes or until vegetables soften. Add mushrooms, bay leaves, and the chopped rosemary; cook, stirring, until fragrant. Stir in tomato paste, stock,

and canned tomatoes; boil. Reduce heat to low; simmer for 25 minutes or until thickened. Add beans and lentils; cook, stirring, for 4 minutes or until beans are tender. Discard bay leaves. Season to taste.
2. Meanwhile, boil, steam, or microwave and sweet potato separately until tender; drain. Mash potato with half the butter until smooth; season. Mash sweet potato with remaining butter until smooth; season.
3. Preheat oven to 210°C/420°F.
4. Spoon lentil mixture evenly into four shallow 2 cups (430ml) ovenproof dishes. Cover filling with both mash mixtures (see tip); sprinkle with parmesan.
5. Bake pies for 25 minutes or until cheese is browned. Serve pies topped with extra rosemary.

Curried Beef and Pea Pie

This delicious and comforting curried beef and pea pie is the perfect dish to make on a cozy night. Combining the savory curry sauce, juicy beef, and sweet peas creates a flavorful balance that will tantalize your taste buds. Plus, this pie is easy-to-make and can be enjoyed by the whole family. Its crunchy pastry crust and warm filling will become one of your favorite dishes. So, what are you waiting for?

15 mins preparation | 50 mins cooking

Ingredients

- 2 tablespoons olive oil
- 2 large brown onions (200g), chopped finely
- 5 clove garlic, crushed
- 620 grams of minced (ground) beef
- 3 tablespoons curry powder
- 3 tablespoons plain (all-purpose) flour
- 3 tablespoons tomato paste
- 2.5 cups beef stock
- 1 cup frozen peas
- 2 sheets of puff pastry
- 2 eggs, beaten lightly

Method

1. Preheat oven to 230°C (210°C fan-forced). Oil 1.5 liters (6-cup) ovenproof dish.
2. Heat oil in a large saucepan; cook onion and garlic, stirring, until onion softens. Add beef; cook, stirring until browned.
3. Add curry powder, and cook, stirring, until fragrant. Add flour; cook, stirring, until the mixture bubbles and thickens. Add paste; gradually stir in stock; stir until mixture boils and thickens; simmer, uncovered, for 12 minutes. Stir in peas; season to taste.
4. Pour mixture into dish. Top with pastry; trim edge. Brush with egg; sprinkle with a little extra curry powder.

5. Bake for about 25 minutes or until pastry is puffed and browned lightly.

Chunky Beef and Vegetable Pie

Ah, the classic comfort food of beef and vegetable pie - nothing beats it! For those who like to cook, this dish is sure to delight. With its hearty chunks of beef and tender vegetables blanketed in a flaky pastry crust, this dish is full of flavor and texture. Whether looking for an easy weeknight meal or a delicious Sunday lunch, this Chunky Beef and Vegetable Pie will surely satisfy your taste buds.

2 hrs 45 mins cooking | Serves 9

Ingredients

- ✓ 2 tablespoons olive oil
- ✓ 2 kilograms gravy beef, cut into 2cm (¾-inch) pieces
- ✓ 65 grams butter
- ✓ 2 medium pieces brown onion (150g), chopped finely
- ✓ 2 clove garlic, crushed
- ✓ 3/4 cup plain (all-purpose) flour
- ✓ 1.5 cups dry white wine
- ✓ 3.5 cups hot beef stock
- ✓ 3 tablespoons tomato paste
- ✓ 3 medium pieces potatoes, cut into 2cm (3/4-inch) pieces
- ✓ 2 large pieces of carrot, cut into 2cm (3/4-inch) pieces
- ✓ 3 stalks of celery, trimmed, cut into 2cm (3/4-inch) pieces
- ✓ 2 large pieces of zucchini, cut into 2cm (3/4-inch) pieces
- ✓ 170 grams (4-1/2 ounces) mushrooms, quartered
- ✓ 1.5 cup (120g) frozen peas
- ✓ 2/3 cup finely chopped fresh flat-leaf parsley
- ✓ 1 2/3 cup plain (all-purpose) flour
- ✓ 2 eggs, beaten lightly
- ✓ 135 grams of cold butter, chopped coarsely
- ✓ 2 eggs yolk
- ✓ 3 tablespoons iced water, approximately

Method

1. Heat oil in a large saucepan; cook beef in batches until browned. Remove from pan.
2. Melt butter in the same pan. Cook onion and garlic, stirring, until onion softens. Add flour, and cook, stirring, until the mixture thickens and bubbles. Gradually stir in wine and stock, and continue stirring until the mixture boils and thickens slightly.
3. Return beef to pan with paste, potato, and carrot, and bring to a boil. Reduce heat, simmer, covered, 1 hour.
4. Meanwhile, make the pastry. Process flour and butter until crumbly. Add egg yolk and enough water until the ingredients come together. Knead dough onto a floured surface until smooth, enclose with plastic wrap, and refrigerate for 30 minutes.
5. Add celery, zucchini, and mushrooms to the beef mixture, simmer, and uncovered for about 35 minutes or until the beef is tender. Remove from heat, and stir in peas and parsley.
6. Preheat oven to 240°C (220°C fan forced).
7. Spoon beef mixture into a deep 3-liter (13-cup) ovenproof dish, and brush the outside edge of the dish with a little egg. Roll pastry between sheets of baking paper until large enough to cover the dish. Lift the pastry over the dish, pressing the edges with a fork to seal. Trim the edge, and brush the pastry with egg.
8. Bake pie for about 25 minutes or until browned.

Beef and Shiitake Mushroom Pie

Beef and Shiitake Mushroom Pie is a delicious and flavorful dish that will please even the pickiest eaters. This unique combination of succulent beef, juicy mushrooms, and a flaky pastry crust is sure to become a family favorite. Whether served as an entree or side dish, this hearty pie will satisfy any craving. With its savory aroma and delectable flavor, the Beef and Shiitake Mushroom Pie will have everyone coming back for seconds.

2 hrs 50 mins cooking | Serves 5

Ingredients

- ✓ 35 grams butter
- ✓ 950 grams of beef brisket, chopped coarsely
- ✓ 3/4 cup plain (all-purpose) flour
- ✓ 3/4 cup light soy sauce
- ✓ 2/3 cup mirin
- ✓ 2/3 cup sake
- ✓ 1.5 cups water
- ✓ 150 grams of oyster mushrooms, chopped coarsely
- ✓ 150 grams of fresh shiitake mushrooms, chopped coarsely
- ✓ 2 sheet puff pastry
- ✓ 2 eggs, beaten lightly
- ✓ 2/3 teaspoon black sesame seeds
- ✓ 2/3 teaspoon white sesame seeds

Method

1. Preheat oven to 170°C (335°F).
2. Melt butter, on the stovetop, in a shallow 22cm flameproof dish; cook beef in batches, stirring, until browned. Return beef to the dish; sprinkle with flour, and stir to combine. Gradually stir in sauce, mirin, sake, and water until smooth. Roast, covered, for 2 hours or until beef is tender. Season to taste.
3. Increase oven to 190°C (370°F).
4. Stir mushrooms into the dish; season. Cover dish with pastry; brush with egg and sprinkle with seeds.

5. Bake pie for 20 minutes or until pastry is browned.

Chicken, Potato, and Leek Pot Pies

Pot pies are a delicious and comforting dish that can be enjoyed all year round. The classic flavors of chicken, potato, and leek are combined for this particular recipe to create an irresistible flavor combination. This combination is then encased in a buttery and flaky crust. The end result is a hearty family-friendly meal that everyone will love. As if the taste wasn't enough, these pot pies can also be made in advance and frozen until ready to bake.

50 mins cooking | Serves 5

Ingredients

- 3 tablespoons olive oil
- 3 bacon slices, trimmed and chopped
- 2 braised leeks, sliced
- 2 clove garlic, crushed
- 2 tablespoons plain flour
- 2.5 cups chicken stock
- 1 cup pouring cream
- 3.5 cups coarsely shredded roast chicken
- 2.5 cups coarsely chopped roast potatoes
- 2 sheets frozen butter puff pastry, partially thawed
- 2 eggs, beaten lightly

Method

1. Heat oil in a large non-stick frying pan over medium heat; cook bacon, stirring, for 3 minutes or until browned. Add leek and garlic; cook for 2 minutes or until garlic is fragrant.
2. Add flour to pan; cook, stirring, for 2 minutes. Gradually whisk in stock. Whisk until the mixture boils and thickens slightly. Whisk in cream; simmer for a further 2 minutes. Remove from heat; season to taste.
3. Transfer mixture to a large heatproof bowl, add chicken and potato; toss well to coat. Refrigerate until cold.
4. Preheat oven to 220°C.

5. Lightly oil four 2 cups ramekins. Cut four rounds from the pastry using the top of a ramekin as a guide. Spoon chicken mixture into ramekins. Place pastry rounds on the chicken mixture; press with a fork to seal the edges. Pierce a small hole in the center of each pastry round; brush with egg.
6. Place ramekins on an oven tray; bake for 30 minutes or until golden and puffed.

Creamy Chicken, Mushroom & Fennel Pie

This Creamy Chicken, Mushroom & Fennel Pie is one of the most comforting and delicious dishes you can make for dinner. The creamy sauce, savory chicken, earthy mushrooms, and fragrant fennel make a divine combination that will have your taste buds singing. Whether for a casual weeknight meal or a special occasion, this pie impresses with its beautiful presentation and robust flavor.

> 50 mins cooking | Serves 5

Ingredients

- ✓ 2 tablespoons olive oil
- ✓ 3 clove garlic, crushed
- ✓ 2 leeks, sliced thinly
- ✓ 2 fennel bulbs, sliced thinly
- ✓ 220 grams swiss brown mushrooms, quartered
- ✓ 2/3 cup dry white wine
- ✓ 5 chicken breasts fillets, chopped coarsely
- ✓ 320 milliliters pouring cream
- ✓ 2 tablespoons Dijon mustard
- ✓ 3/4 cup fresh flat-leaf parsley, coarsely chopped
- ✓ 3 sheets of puff pastry
- ✓ 2 eggs, beaten lightly
- ✓ 2 tablespoons fennel seeds
- ✓ 2/3 teaspoon sea salt flakes

Method

1. Preheat oven to 220°C (190°C fan forced).
2. Heat oil in a large saucepan over medium heat. Cook garlic, leek, fennel, and mushrooms, stirring, for 7 minutes or until vegetables soften.
3. Stir in wine, and bring to a boil. Reduce heat, and simmer for 4 minutes. Add chicken and cream, and bring to a boil. Reduce heat, and simmer for 15 minutes or until chicken is cooked through and the sauce has thickened slightly. Stir in mustard and parsley.

4. Spoon filling into four 2 cups of ovenproof bowls or dishes. Cut pastry sheets in half, and trim halves into 12cm x 18cm (4-3/4-inch x 7-1/4-inch) rectangles. Place a pastry rectangle on each bowl, pressing down gently to seal. Brush pastry with egg. Using a small sharp knife, score five lines on each pastry lid at 2.5cm (1-inch) intervals; sprinkle tops with fennel seeds and salt.
5. Bake pies for 30 minutes or until the pastry is puffed and golden.

Steak and Kidney Pie

Steak and kidney pie is one of the most popular dishes in the UK. It is a hearty meal, combining salty steak with savory kidneys in a delicious gravy encased in buttery, flaky pastry. This traditional dish has been around for centuries, evolving to become an iconic part of British cuisine. Steak and Kidney Pie will satisfy you whether you are looking for a comfort food classic or something new.

30 mins preparation | 2 hrs 35 mins cooking

Ingredients

- ✓ 320 grams lamb's kidneys, trimmed, quartered
- ✓ 2 tablespoons Worcestershire sauce
- ✓ 3 tablespoons vegetable oil
- ✓ 1.5 kilograms gravy beef, trimmed, cubed
- ✓ 3/4 cup plain seasoned flour
- ✓ 3 onions, chopped
- ✓ 3 garlic cloves, crushed
- ✓ 1.5 cups beef stock
- ✓ 1.5 cups water
- ✓ 2/3 cup red wine
- ✓ bouquet garni

Rough puff pastry

- ✓ 1 cup plain flour
- ✓ 270 grams of butter, chopped, at room temperature
- ✓ 2/3 cup cold water
- ✓ 2 eggs, lightly beaten

Method

1. In a bowl, combine kidneys and sauce. Heat half the oil in a heavy-based saucepan on medium. Saute kidneys until lightly browned. Set aside.

2. Heat the remaining oil in the same pan. Dust beef in flour, shaking off excess. Cook in two batches for 7 minutes, until well browned. Transfer to a plate.
3. In the same pan, saute onion and garlic for 4 minutes, until tender. Return kidneys and beef to pan with stock, water, wine, and bouquet garni. Bring to a boil. Reduce heat to low. Cook, covered, for 1 hour. Uncover and simmer for 45 minutes until the sauce thickens.
4. Make pastry using the method below.
5. Preheat oven to very hot, 230°C. Spoon meat and gravy into a 7-cup ovenproof dish.
6. Roll out the pastry to 5mm thick. Cut to cover the top of the dish. Brush with egg. Cut 5 slits on top of the pie. Place on an oven tray. Bake for 15 minutes. Reduce oven to moderate, 180°C. Bake for further 25 minutes, until crisp and golden. Serve with the veggies of your choice.

Pastry

1. Sift flour into a bowl. Add butter. Rub in until almost combined. Add water, and mix to a streaky dough. Roll out on floured board to 20 x 50cm. Fold into thirds. Give a quarter-turn and roll again. Repeat twice. Cut in halves. Wrap in plastic wrap, and chill half for 35 minutes (freeze the remainder for later use).

Spanish Chicken Pie

Spanish Chicken Pie is a savory and delicious dish perfect for any occasion. It's made with aromatic spices, juicy chicken, and hearty vegetables, all cooked in a crispy golden crust. This dish is easy to make and can be enjoyed by the whole family. Not only does it taste great, but it also has a unique flavor that will leave you wanting more. It will become a favorite in your home with just the right amount of spice.

1 hr 40 mins cooking | Serves 5

Ingredients

- 180 grams of cured chorizo sausage, sliced thinly
- 650 grams of chicken thigh fillets, chopped coarsely
- 2 red onions, chopped coarsely
- 3 celery stalks, trimmed, chopped coarsely
- 270 gram roasted red capsicum, chopped coarsely
- 2 fennel bulbs, cut and sliced thinly
- 3 clove garlic, crushed
- 2/3 teaspoon saffron threads
- 4 teaspoons mild paprika
- 3/4 cup tomato paste
- 1 cup water
- 2/3 cup seeded black olives
- 3 potatoes, unpeeled, sliced thinly

Method

2. Heat a large saucepan; cook chorizo, turning, until crisp. Remove from pan. Cook chicken in batches until browned all over. Remove from pan.
3. Add onion, celery, capsicum, fennel, and garlic to pan; cook, stirring, until softened. Add saffron, paprika, paste, and water; boil. Return chicken and chorizo to the pan. Reduce heat, and simmer, uncovered, for about 20 minutes or until chicken is cooked through and sauce thickens. Stir in olives. Transfer to a 1.5-liter (6-cup) ovenproof dish.

4. Meanwhile, preheat the oven to 230°C/435°F. Arrange potato slices, slightly overlapping, over the chicken mixture. Bake, uncovered, for about 50 minutes or until potatoes are tender.

Chicken and Mushroom Pot Pies

Chicken and Mushroom Pot Pies are a classic comfort food dish that is delicious and easy to make. They can be made in individual servings and in a large family-sized version to feed a crowd. These savory pies feature a variety of flavorful ingredients, such as mushrooms, chicken, onions, carrots, and herbs, all wrapped up in a buttery homemade pie crust.

> 1.30 hr cooking | Serves 5

Ingredients

- ✓ 2.5 cups salt-reduced chicken stock
- ✓ 1 cup dry white wine
- ✓ 550 grams of chicken breast fillets
- ✓ 45 grams butter
- ✓ 2 clove garlic, crushed
- ✓ 2 small leeks, halved, thinly sliced
- ✓ 3 stalks of celery, trimmed, thinly sliced
- ✓ 9 medium cups mushroom, thinly sliced
- ✓ 3/4 cup plain flour
- ✓ 2/3 cup cream
- ✓ salt, freshly ground black pepper, to taste
- ✓ 3 sheets of ready-rolled butter puff pastry
- ✓ 2 tablespoons milk
- ✓ 5 cups mushrooms, extra

Method

1. Chicken and mushroom pot pies
2. Combine stock and wine in a medium saucepan; bring to a boil.
3. Add chicken; simmer gently, uncovered, for 10 minutes, turning halfway during cooking. Remove from heat; allow the chicken to cool in the liquid. Remove chicken from pan; chop coarsely.
4. Bring liquid to boil; boil, uncovered, for about 5 minutes or until reduced to 1 2/3 cups.

5. In a large saucepan, melt butter. Add garlic, leek, celery, and mushrooms; cook, stirring, for about 7 minutes, or until softened. Add flour; cook, stirring, about 2 minutes or until bubbly.
6. Gradually add stock mixture; constantly stir until the mixture boils and thickens. Stir in cream; return chicken to sauce. Season to taste with salt and pepper.
7. Preheat oven to hot, 220°C (190°C fan-forced).
8. Divide chicken mixture among 4 x 1 1/4-cup (310ml) capacity ovenproof dishes. Cut pastry to fit the tops of dishes and slightly overlap. Brush the pastry with milk; place an extra mushroom on top of each pastry square.
9. Place dishes on an oven tray. Bake for about 25 minutes or until the pastry is puffed and browned.

Curried Chicken Pies

If you're looking for a savory, flavorful dish that will please everyone around the dinner table, look no further than curried chicken pies! This easy-to-make dish combines traditional Indian flavors with a classic British pastry to create an exciting, delicious meal. The combination of spices in the curry creates a tantalizing aroma that will fill your home and bring everyone running to the kitchen!

2 hrs 35 mins cooking | Serves 7

Ingredients

- ✓ 1.7 kilograms chicken
- ✓ 95 grams butter
- ✓ 1.5 white onion, chopped finely
- ✓ 3 stalks of celery, trimmed, chopped finely
- ✓ 1.5 leeks, chopped finely
- ✓ 1.5 red capsicums (bell pepper), chopped finely
- ✓ 4 teaspoons curry powder
- ✓ 3/4 teaspoon chili powder
- ✓ 3/4 cup plain (all-purpose) flour
- ✓ 2/3 cup sour cream
- ✓ 2/3 cup fresh flat-leaf parsley, finely chopped
- ✓ 3 (sheets) of puff pastry
- ✓ 2 eggs, beaten lightly

Method

1. Place chicken in a large saucepan with enough water to cover the chicken, and bring it to a boil. Reduce heat, simmer, uncovered, 1 hour. Remove pan from heat. When cool enough to handle, remove the chicken from the stock. Reserve 2 cups (440ml) of the stock for this recipe.
2. Preheat oven to 220°C (190°C fan forced).
3. Remove skin and bones from chicken, and coarsely chop chicken flesh.

4. Heat butter in a large frying pan. Cook onion, celery, leek, and capsicum, stirring, until vegetables are soft.
5. Add curry powder and chili powder, and cook until fragrant. Stir in flour. Add reserved stock, stir over heat until mixture boils and thickens, reduce heat, simmer for 2 minutes, and remove from heat. Stir in sour cream, chopped chicken, and parsley. Spoon mixture into six 1 3/4-cup ovenproof dishes.
6. Cut pastry into six large rounds to cover each dish's top. Lightly brush pastry with egg. Place pies on the oven tray.
7. Bake for 15 minutes. Reduce oven to 190°C (170°C fan forced), and bake pies for 20 minutes or until pastry is golden brown.

Fish Pot Pies

Fish pot pies are an easy and delicious meal that can be enjoyed any time of the year. They are satisfying and comforting, yet also creative and varied. With the right ingredients and a few simple steps, anyone can make a tasty fish pot pie in the comfort of their own home. Whether you use fresh fish or canned varieties, there's plenty of opportunity to mix up different flavors.

55 mins cooking | Serves 5

Ingredients

- 1.5 cups fish stock
- 1 cup water
- 350 grams salmon fillets, cut into 2cm pieces
- 350 grams firm white fish fillets, cut into 2cm pieces
- 3 large potatoes, chopped coarsely
- 2 small kumaras, chopped coarsely
- 3 tablespoon milk
- 45 grams butter
- 3 tablespoons plain flour
- 2 tablespoons finely chopped fresh flat-leaf parsley
- 2/3 cup coarsely grated cheddar cheese

Method

1. Place stock and the water in a medium saucepan and boil. Add fish, reduce heat; simmer gently, about 3 minutes or until cooked through. Remove fish from pan; place a few pieces each of salmon and white fish in 1.5 cups shallow ovenproof dish for toddlers, then divide remaining fish into three 3-cup shallow ovenproof dishes. Strain the stock mixture into the medium jug; discard the solids.
2. Boil, steam, or microwave vegetables until tender; drain. Push vegetables through the sieve into a large bowl; stir in milk and half the butter until smooth. Cover to keep warm.
3. Preheat grill.

4. Melt remaining butter in a small saucepan; add flour, and cook, stirring, about 3 minutes or until the mixture bubbles and thickens. Gradually stir in the reserved stock mixture; cook until the sauce boils and thickens. Stir in parsley.
5. Pour a little sauce over the toddler's fish; top with some vegetable mixture.
6. Pour remaining sauce over fish in large dishes, top with remaining vegetable mixture; season to taste.
7. Sprinkle dishes with cheese. Place dishes on oven tray; grill until browned lightly.

Chicken Pot Pie

Chicken Pot Pie is a classic comfort food that warms the soul. It's a timeless family favorite that can be prepared in many ways. Whether you make it from scratch or use store-bought ingredients, this savory dish will easily become a regular on your dinner rotation. With its flaky crust and flavorful filling of vegetables, chicken, herbs, and spices, Chicken Pot Pie will leave everyone at the table satisfied and happy.

25 mins preparation | 45 mins cooking | Serves 5

Ingredients

- ✓ 650 grams of chicken breast fillets, chopped coarsely
- ✓ 25 grams butter, plus 45 g extra
- ✓ 450 grams of kumara, chopped finely
- ✓ 2 medium leeks, sliced
- ✓ 2 clove garlic, crushed
- ✓ 3 tablespoons plain flour
- ✓ 2/3 cup chicken stock
- ✓ 3/4 cup cream
- ✓ 2 tablespoons chopped chives
- ✓ 3 sheets butter puff pastry
- ✓ 2 eggs, beaten lightly

Method

1. Melt 25 grams of butter in a large frying pan over medium heat; add kumara and leek. Cook, occasionally stirring, until tender. Transfer to a large bowl
2. Using the same pan, add chicken and garlic. Cook chicken for 5 minutes on each side until browned and almost cooked. Add to kumara mixture.
3. In a separate smaller pan, melt the remaining butter. Add flour; cook, stirring, until the mixture bubbles. Gradually stir in the stock. Bring to a boil; simmer, stirring, until thickened. Stir in cream and chives.

4. Add sauce to the chicken mixture. Spread into a greased, shallow 23cm-square ovenproof dish with a rim. Stand separate pastry sheets on the kitchen bench for 7 minutes or until partially thawed. Preheat the oven to 250°C (190°C fan-forced).
5. Cut three 1cm strips from one sheet of pastry. Brush the rim of the dish with a little water; press pastry strips onto the rim of the dish, and join strips with a little water. Top the pie with the second pastry sheet, pressing firmly to seal the pastry together. Trim edge.
6. Brush pastry with egg, and place dish on an oven tray. Bake for 35 minutes or until browned.

Chicken, Leek, and Pumpkin Pot Pies

Nothing is quite as comforting as a hot, freshly cooked pot pie. Chicken, leek, and pumpkin pot pies offer a delicious and unique spin on a classic dish. This perfect combination of flavors creates the ultimate comfort food experience that will leave your family wanting more. These pot pies are easy to prepare and can be made in advance, so you can enjoy them any time without too much fuss. Read on to discover how to make a delicious chicken, leek, and pumpkin pot pie.

20 mins preparation | 30 mins cooking | Serves 5

Ingredients

- ✓ 550 grams of chicken breast fillets, cut into 2cm cubes
- ✓ 3 tablespoons plain flour
- ✓ 3 tablespoons olive oil
- ✓ 2 leeks, pale section only, thinly sliced
- ✓ 3 clove garlic, crushed
- ✓ 3 tablespoon mustard powder
- ✓ 1-3/4 cup dry white wine
- ✓ 2 large salt-reduced chicken stock cube
- ✓ 500 grams jap pumpkin, peeled, cut into 2cm pieces
- ✓ 350 milliliters of reduced-fat thickened cream
- ✓ 150 grams green beans, topped, cut into 2cm lengths
- ✓ 1-395g block frozen butter puff pastry, thawed
- ✓ 2 eggs lightly beaten

Method

1. Toss chicken in flour to lightly coat. Heat half the oil in a large frying pan on medium.
2. Cook chicken in batches, 4 minutes for each batch, or until golden brown. Transfer to a large bowl.
3. Add remaining oil to pan. Cook leek for 4 mins or until softened slightly. Add garlic and mustard; cook, stirring, for 35 seconds or until fragrant.

4. Add wine and bring to a boil. Reduce heat. Crumble in the stock cube; stir in the pumpkin. Simmer, covered, for 5 minutes or until the pumpkin is almost tender.
5. Stir cream, beans, and chicken through the pumpkin mixture. Bring to a simmer; simmer, uncovered, for 4 minutes, or until chicken is cooked and beans are bright green and tender. Season to taste.
6. Spoon mixture into 4 x 1 1/2 cup-capacity ovenproof dishes.
7. Preheat oven to very hot, 240°C (220°C fan-forced).
8. Roll the pastry out to a 24 x 30cm rectangle. Cut four discs from the pastry using a 12cm round pastry cutter. Cut four leaf shapes from pastry off-cuts.
9. Place pastry discs on top of each ramekin. Top each with a pastry leaf. Brush with egg.
10. Bake pies for 17 minutes, until puffed and golden brown. Serve.

Fish Pie with Potato and Celeriac Mash

Fish Pie with Potato and Celeriac Mash is a comforting and delicious combination of flavors that makes for a hearty meal. This classic dish is sure to delight the entire family, from young kids to adults. This dish is full of texture and flavor with its creamy mashed potato topping, deliciously flaky fish, and crunchy celeriac mash base.

30 mins preparation | 45 mins cooking | Serves 7

Ingredients

- 2 medium celeriac, peeled, chopped coarsely
- 5 medium desire potatoes, peeled, chopped coarsely
- 30 grams butter
- 3/4 cup milk, warmed
- salt and freshly ground white pepper
- 95 grams of butter, extra
- 4 small leeks, sliced thickly
- 3/4 cup plain flour
- 1-2/3 cup milk
- 1.5 kilograms of boneless white fish fillets, chopped coarsely
- 3 teaspoons lemon juice
- 3/4 cup coarsely chopped fresh chives

Method

1. Boil or steam the celeriac and potato until soft; drain. Mash the celeriac and potato with butter and warmed milk until smooth. Season to taste with salt and pepper.
2. Meanwhile, heat 65g of the extra butter in a large saucepan, add the leeks, and cook, covered, until soft. Add the flour, and cook, stirring, for about 3 minutes. Gradually stir in the milk; bring to a boil, occasionally stirring.
3. Add the fish to the pan; simmer, covered, for 4 minutes. Gently stir in lemon juice and chives without breaking up the fish.
4. Preheat the oven to hot, 240°C (220°C fan-forced). Spoon the fish mixture into an ovenproof dish (2.5 liters/10-cups capacity). Melt

the remaining butter. Top fish mixture with potato and celeriac mash; brush top liberally with melted butter. Place the dish on an oven tray.
5. Bake the pie in a hot oven for about 30 minutes or until golden brown.

Veal Pie with Cheesy Semolina Topping

Veal Pie with Cheesy Semolina Topping is an irresistible dish that will make your taste buds tingle. This delicious dish will be the highlight of any meal by combining succulent veal with a rich, flavorful sauce and topped with a golden, cheesy semolina topping. Whether you are hosting a formal dinner party or simply looking for something special to serve your family during the holidays, Veal Pie with Cheesy Semolina Topping is sure to impress.

30 mins preparation | 2 hrs 30 mins cooking | Serves 7

Ingredients

Veal pie

- 1.5 kilograms of diced veal
- 2/3 cup plain flour
- 3/4 cup olive oil
- 3 clove garlic, crushed
- 3 small brown onions chopped coarsely
- 3 medium carrots, chopped coarsely
- 3 trimmed celery stalks, chopped coarsely
- 2/3 cup white wine
- 450 gram can diced tomatoes, undrained
- 2.5 cup chicken stock
- 25 grams butter, melted

Gremolata

- 2 cloves garlic, chopped finely
- 3 tablespoons finely chopped fresh flat-leaf parsley
- 2 tablespoons grated lemon rind

Cheesy semolina

- 3.5 cups milk
- 2 teaspoons salt
- ground nutmeg
- 1 cup semolina

- ✓ 1-3/4 cup finely grated
- ✓ parmesan cheese
- ✓ 2 eggs, beaten lightly

Method

1. Toss veal in flour; shake away excess. Heat 3 tablespoons of oil in a large flameproof casserole dish; cook veal in batches until browned.
2. Heat the remaining oil in the same dish; cook garlic, onion, carrots, and celery, stirring, until soft. Add wine, and boil until almost evaporated. Return veal to the pan with tomatoes and stock; boil. Simmer for 50 minutes, covered, and uncovered for an additional hour until tender.
3. For the gremolata, combine all ingredients in a small bowl.
4. For cheesy semolina, combine milk, salt, and nutmeg in a medium pan and boil. Reduce heat, and gradually stir in the semolina. Stir over low heat for 7 minutes or until thick. Remove from heat, and stir in 1 cup (80g) of the cheese and the egg. Use immediately.
5. Preheat oven to moderately hot, 220°C (190°C fan-forced). Place veal mixture in a 2.5 liter (10-cup) ovenproof dish. Sprinkle with half the gremolata and cover with cheesy semolina. Brush with butter and sprinkle with remaining cheese. Bake for 30 minutes or until the top is browned lightly. Serve with remaining gremolata.

Printed in Great Britain
by Amazon